American Indian

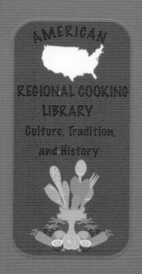

AMERICAN

REGIONAL COOKING
LIBRARY
Culture, Tradition,
and History

American Indian

Mason Crest Publishers

Philadelphia

Mason Crest Publishers Inc.
370 Reed Road
Broomall, Pennsylvania 19008
(866) MCP-BOOK (toll free)
www.masoncrest.com

First printing
1 2 3 4 5 6 7 8 9 10
Library of Congress Cataloging-in-Publication Data

Sanna, Ellyn, 1958-
   American Indian / compiled by Ellyn Sanna.
       p. cm. — (American regional cooking library)
   Includes index.
   ISBN 1-59084-611-7
   1. Indian cookery—Juvenile literature. 2. Cookery, American—Juvenile literature. I. Title.
II. Series.
   TX715.S1452423 2005
   641.59'297—dc22
                                    2004016730

Recipes prepared and tested by Marsha McIntosh.
Recipes contributed by Alfred Herron.
Produced by Harding House Publishing Services, Inc., Vestal, New York.
Interior design by Dianne Hodack.
Cover design by Michelle Bouch.
Printed and bound in the Hashemite Kingdom of Jordan.

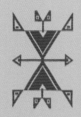

Contents

Introduction
by the Culinary Institute of America

Cooking is a dynamic profession, one that presents some of the greatest challenges and offers some of the greatest rewards. Since 1946, the Culinary Institute of America has provided aspiring and seasoned food service professionals with the knowledge and skills needed to become leaders and innovators in this industry.

Here at the CIA, we teach our students the fundamental culinary techniques they need to build a sound foundation for their food service careers. There is always another level of perfection for them to achieve and another skill to master. Our rigorous curriculum provides them with a springboard to continued growth and success.

Food is far more than simply sustenance or the source of energy to fuel you and your family through life's daily regimen. It conjures memories throughout life, summoning up the smell, taste, and flavor of simpler times. Cooking is more than an art and a science; it provides family history. Food prepared with care epitomizes the love, devotion, and culinary delights that you offer to your friends and family.

A cuisine provides a way to express and establish customs—the way a food should taste and the flavors and aromas associated with that food. Cuisines are more than just a collection of ingredients, cooking utensils, and dishes from a geographic location; they are elements that are critical to establishing a culinary identity.

When you can accurately read a recipe, you can trace a variety of influences by observing which ingredients are selected and also by noting the technique that is used. If you research the historical origins of a recipe, you may find ingredients that traveled from East to West or from the New World to the Old. Traditional methods of cooking a dish may have changed with the times or to meet special challenges.

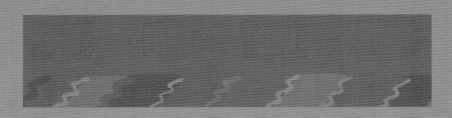

The history of cooking illustrates the significance of innovation and the trading or sharing of ingredients and tools between societies. Although the various cooking vessels over the years have changed, the basic cooking methods have remained the same. Through adaptation, a recipe created years ago in a remote corner of the world could today be recognized by many throughout the globe.

When observing the customs of different societies, it becomes apparent that food brings people together. It is the common thread that we share and that we value. Regardless of the occasion, food is present to celebrate and to comfort. Through food we can experience other cultures and lands, learning the significance of particular ingredients and cooking techniques.

As you begin your journey through the culinary arts, keep in mind the power that food and cuisine holds. When passed from generation to generation, family heritage and traditions remain strong. Become familiar with the dishes your family has enjoyed through the years and play a role in keeping them alive. Don't be afraid to embellish recipes along the way – creativity is what cooking is all about.

American Indian Culture, History, and Traditions

Centuries ago, when Europeans first arrived in North America, they found other human beings already living here. These groups of people—called "Indians" because when Christopher Columbus first landed in the Americas, he thought he had reached India—had a very different worldview than the white newcomers did.

Although many tribes, many languages, and many cultures fall under the heading of "American Indian," all these people shared some things in common. One of the most important is their attitude toward the Earth. For them, the Earth is a loving mother who provides human beings with bountiful nourishment. All food comes from her hand.

Of course Europeans also understood that food comes from the Earth, but they saw the Earth as being there for human beings' convenience, while food was the product of people's hard work. They did not feel the same sense of respect and intimacy that Native people felt for their "mother." Instead, Europeans often had a more adversarial relationship with the land; it was something to be conquered with courage and determined labor.

But Native Americans had a close friendship with the natural world around them. They had lived with their "mother" for centuries, and they had learned much from her. She was not their adversary; instead, with open hands, she offered them an abundance of foods.

As you look at these American Indian recipes, you should be able to recognize the ways they express the Indians' ongoing and practical dependence on the Earth. You may also see the ways that Indian food traditions have influenced the food we eat today. We owe much to the Native people of this continent, whose wisdom and insights helped shape the early European settlers' experience.

And the influence of American Indians is still a real part of the world where you live today. In fact, some food experts indicate that 60 percent of modern foods around the world came from the Native people of the Americas!

Before you cook...

If you haven't done much cooking before, you may find recipe books a little confusing. Certain words and terms can seem unfamiliar. You may find the measurements difficult to understand. What appears to be an easy or familiar dish may contain ingredients you've never heard of before. You might not understand what utensil the recipe calls for you to use, or you might not be sure what the recipe is asking you to do.

Reading the pages in this section before you get started may help you understand the directions better so that your cooking goes more smoothly. You can also refer back to these pages whenever you run into questions.

Safety Tips

Cooking involves handling very hot and very sharp objects, so being careful is common sense. What's more, you want to be certain that anything you plan on putting in your mouth is safe to eat. If you follow these easy tips, you should find that cooking can be both fun and safe.

Before you cook...

- Always wash your hands before and after handling food. This is particularly important after you handle raw meats, poultry, and eggs, as bacteria called salmonella can live on these uncooked foods. You can't see or smell salmonella, but these germs can make you or anyone who swallows them very sick.
- Make a habit of using potholders or oven mitts whenever you handle pots and pans from the oven or microwave.
- Always set pots, pans, and knives with their handles away from counter edges. This way you won't risk catching your sleeves on them—and any younger children in the house won't be in danger of grabbing something hot or sharp.
- Don't leave perishable food sitting out of the refrigerator for more than an hour or two.
- Wash all raw fruits and vegetables to remove dirt and chemicals.
- Use a cutting board when chopping vegetables or fruit, and always cut away from yourself.
- Don't overheat grease or oil—but if grease or oil does catch fire, don't try to extinguish the flames with water. Instead, throw baking soda or salt on the fire to put it out. Turn all stove burners off.
- If you burn yourself, immediately put the burn under cold water, as this will prevent the burn from becoming more painful.
- Never put metal dishes or utensils in the microwave. Use only microwave-proof dishes.
- Wash cutting boards and knives thoroughly after cutting meat, fish or poultry — especially when raw and before using the same tools to prepare other foods such as vegetables and cheese. This will prevent the spread of bacteria such as salmonella.
- Keep your hands away from any moving parts of appliances, such as mixers.
- Unplug any appliance, such as a mixer, blender, or food processor before assembling for use or disassembling after use.

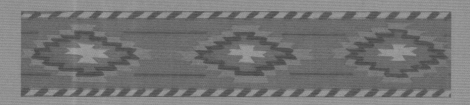

Metric Conversion Table

Most cooks in the United States use measuring containers based on an eight-ounce cup, a teaspoon, and a tablespoon. Meanwhile, cooks in Canada and Europe are more apt to use metric measurements. The recipes in this book use cups, teaspoons, and tablespoons—but you can convert these measurements to metric by using the table below.

Temperature
To convert Fahrenheit degrees to Celsius, subtract 32 and multiply by .56.

212°F = 100°C
(this is the boiling point of water)
250°F = 110°C
275°F = 135°C
300°F = 150°C
325°F = 160°C
350°F = 180°C
375°F = 190°C
400°F = 200°C

Liquid Measurements
1 teaspoon = 5 milliliters
1 tablespoon = 15 milliliters
1 fluid ounce = 30 milliliters
1 cup = 240 milliliters
1 pint = 480 milliliters
1 quart = 0.95 liters
1 gallon = 3.8 liters

Measurements of Mass or Weight
1 ounce = 28 grams
8 ounces = 227 grams
1 pound (16 ounces) = 0.45 kilograms
2.2 pounds = 1 kilogram

Measurements of Length
¼ inch = 0.6 centimeters
½ inch = 1.25 centimeters
1 inch = 2.5 centimeters

Pan Sizes

Baking pans are usually made in standard sizes. The pans used in the United States are roughly equivalent to the following metric pans:

9-inch cake pan = 23-centimeter pan
11x7-inch baking pan = 28x18-centimeter baking pan
13x9-inch baking pan = 32.5x23-centimeter baking pan
9x5-inch loaf pan = 23x13-centimeter loaf pan
2-quart casserole = 2-liter casserole

Useful Tools, Utensils, Dishes

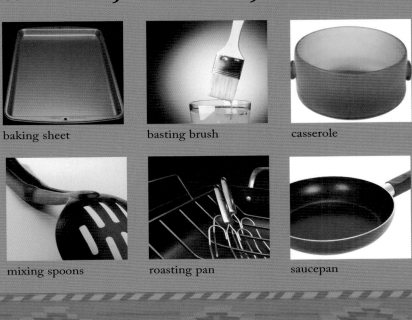

baking sheet   basting brush   casserole

mixing spoons   roasting pan   saucepan

Cooking Glossary

baste To brush or spoon pan drippings or other fat or liquid over food as it cooks.

blanch To immerse food briefly in boiling water.

cream To combine butter and sugar. This works best when the butter is room temperature, so take the butter out of the refrigerator at least an hour before you want to use it.

cut To mix dry ingredients and butter or hard shortening with a fork or pastry cutter.

fold Gently combine a lighter substance with a heavier batter by spooning the lighter mixture through the heavier one without using strong beating strokes.

giblets The edible internal organs of fowl.

knead To work dough with hands in a fold-and-press motion.

pinch An amount that equals less than 1/4 teaspoon.

simmer Gently boil, so that the surface of the liquid just ripples gently.

toss Turn food over quickly and lightly so that it is evenly covered with a liquid or powder.

truss To bind poultry for roasting with string or skewers.

Special American Indian Flavors

berries

nuts

honey

wild greens

American Indian Recipes

Salmon Soup (Pacific Northwest)

Ingredients:

6 cups chicken broth
½ pound canned salmon
⅔ cup sliced green onions
a pinch of salt and pepper
½ cup watercress
½ cup small-leaf spinach

Cooking utensils you'll need:
measuring cups
saucepan

Directions:

Combine chicken broth, salmon, and green onions in a large saucepan and bring to a boil. Reduce heat, cover, and *simmer* for 15 minutes. Add salt, pepper, watercress, and spinach. Cook an additional 5 minutes. Makes 6 servings.

American Indian Food History and Tradition

When was the last time you said thank you to the cow that provided the hamburger you were about to eat? Maybe never. Most Americans don't think of the intimate connections between human beings and animals; we think of ground beef as coming in a plastic-wrapped package; and we may feel uncomfortable thinking of the animals whose bodies we eat.

But Native Americans often look at their food a bit differently. Each year when the first salmon ran up the streams, they were greeted with a ritual of thanksgiving. The wife of the fisherman who caught the first fish might recite this prayer:

O supernatural ones! O swimmers! I thank you that you are willing to come to us. Protect us from danger that nothing evil may happen to us when we eat you. . . . For that is the reason you come here that we may catch you for food. We know that only your bodies are dead here, but your souls come to watch over us when we are going to eat what you have given us.

For centuries, the Haida, Tlingit, Tsimshian, and Bella Bella people have eaten salmon with great gratitude. During the spring and summer, five kinds of salmon run up the rivers from the ocean. These Indians built their villages along the coast, and today, they still rely on the sea for their food. In the past, food was so abundant that these people "harvested" the world around them in much the same way a farmer harvests crops.

American Indian Food History and Traditions

In the Pacific Northwest, wild geese come down from Canada for the winter, providing the Northwest tribes with a tasty dish that's a change from salmon.

European traders and missionaries were the first to bring both brown and white sugar to the Tlingit of the Northwest. Brown sugar was kept in solid cakes and then boiled down into a syrup. Lumps of brown sugar were often served at feasts.

These great feasts were a common event in Northwest Native culture. Referred to as a "potlatch" (a Chinook word meaning "gift"), entire villages for miles around would be invited to such a feast. It was an occasion to share the abundant food nature had provided.

Roasted Goose (Pacific Northwest)

Preheat oven to 350 degrees Fahrenheit.

Ingredients:

1 8-pound goose
2 teaspoons ground ginger
salt and pepper
2 cups chopped, dried apples
1 cup dried cranberries
½ cup dried currants (optional)
¾ cup brown sugar
2 tablespoons water

Cooking utensils you'll need:
measuring cups
mixing bowl
measuring spoons
roasting pan
saucepan
mixing spoons
basting brush

Directions:

Rinse the goose, and then allow the fat to drain off by pricking the skin along the breast and thighs. Brush on 1 teaspoon of the ginger and sprinkle it with the salt and pepper. Combine the rest of the ginger with the dried fruits in a bowl and stuff the goose with this mixture. *Truss* the goose if you want. Put the goose in the oven and allow it to roast for 15-25 minutes for each pound. When you prick a thigh with a knife or fork and the juice runs clear, the meat is cooked.

During the last hour of cooking time, *baste* the goose with brown sugar sauce. This sauce is made by combining brown sugar and water in a small saucepan and heating it over medium heat until the mixture boils. Keep stirring it for 2 minutes afterward and then remove from the heat.

Before carving the goose, make sure it has sat and cooled for at least 15 minutes.

Iroquois Soup (Northeast)

Ingredients:

4 cups chicken broth
1 cup chopped onions
2 tablespoons cornmeal
¾ pound haddock, trout, or bass fillets
1 ½ cups frozen lima beans
4–6 mushrooms, sliced thin
2 tablespoons chopped fresh parsley
2 tablespoons chopped fresh dill
salt and pepper

Cooking utensils you'll need:
measuring cups
measuring spoons
sharp knife for cutting parsley,
dill, onions, and mushrooms
saucepan

Directions:

Simmer broth, onions, and cornmeal in a large saucepan over low heat. Add fish, lima beans, and mushrooms; continue cooking for 25 minutes, stirring occasionally and breaking the fish into small pieces. Add parsley and dill and cook for a minute more. Season to taste with salt and pepper and serve. Makes 4 to 6 servings.

American Indian Food History and Traditions

The powerful Iroquois Confederacy—the Mohawk, Onondaga, Cayuga, Oneida, and Seneca—was based in what is now New York State, but its influence extended north, west, and south. These people were politically wise, with a sophisticated culture, and their lives followed nature's cycles: hunting, gathering, and farming, eating from each season's bounty. The cycle was marked by ceremonies of thanksgiving, occasions when the Iroquois expressed their gratitude for the nourishment the Earth provided.

American Indian History and Traditions

The Northeastern tribes were farmers as well as hunters. They planted sunflower seeds around their gardens, valuing the plant for its beauty, as well as the nourishment it provided.

Sunflower seeds are a good source of protein. Northeastern Indians cooked them (as in this recipe), but these tribes also pressed sunflower seeds to make oil; ground them into butter for cooking; and roasted them to make a beverage something like coffee. They also ate handfuls as a snack. (And you may enjoy them this way too!)

Sunflower Seed Soup (Northeast)

Ingredients:

2 cups hulled sunflower seeds
6 cups chicken broth
3 small green onions, thinly sliced
2 tablespoons chopped fresh dill
salt and pepper to taste

Cooking utensils you'll need:
measuring cups
measuring spoons
saucepan

Directions:

Put the sunflower seeds in a saucepan with the chicken broth and onions. Leave uncovered and cook over low heat for about an hour; then stir in the dill and season with salt and pepper, and serve.

Maple Baked Beans (Northeast)

Ingredients:

1 pound dried navy, kidney, baby lima, pinto, or black beans
4 to 6 strips thick–sliced bacon
½ cup maple syrup
½ cup molasses
1 teaspoon dry mustard
salt (optional)

Cooking utensils you'll need:
measuring cups
measuring spoons
large pot
baking dish
mixing bowl

Directions:

Place the beans in the pot and cover them with water, allow them to soak overnight and in the morning drain and cover them with cold fresh water. Cook the beans in the liquid over low heat for 2 to 3 hours, or until they're tender. To keep the beans from sticking, add more water as needed. After the beans are cooked, drain the water. Place the bacon on the sides and bottom of baking dish. Combine the beans, syrup, molasses, and mustard in the mixing bowl, along with some salt if desire. Pour this mixture into the baking dish and bake covered for 2 hours at 300 degrees Fahrenheit. Stir occasionally, and after the 2 hours, uncover and cook for 30 minutes longer.

Tip:

You can make this recipe in a slow cooker instead of on the stovetop and in the oven. Plan on allowing the beans to cook most of the day at high heat.

American Indian Food History and Tradition

The long-ago Indian cooks who made this dish didn't have ovens or stoves—so they dug pits in the earth, lined them with stones that had been heated in a fire, and buried pots of food in the pits. Then they left the food to simmer for many hours, until it was tender and well-cooked.

Before the coming of the Europeans, maple sugar was the only sweetener used by the Eastern tribes. Each spring, when the maple sap began to run, the Northeastern people gave thanks for this sweet food at their Maple Festival, a time of celebration, food, and worship.

Succotash (Northeast)

Ingredients:

Cooking utensils you'll need:
measuring cups
saucepan

4 ears of sweet corn
3 to 4 cups fresh or 2 10-ounce packages frozen lima beans
1½ cups water
¼ cup butter
salt and ground pepper
1⅓ cups sliced green onions
1 green and 1 red bell pepper (or 2 green) seeded and diced

Directions:

Cut the corncobs into 1½ inch-long pieces. Place these, along with the beans, water, and butter, in a saucepan, along with salt and pepper for seasoning. Cover the pan and cook over high heat until the water boils. Then lower the heat and *simmer* for 10 minutes. Add the peppers and green onions and continue to simmer until the beans are tender. Then remove the lid and cook on high for 3-4 minutes until there is only about ½ cup of liquid left in the pan.

American Indian Food History and Tradition

Corn and beans (along with squash) were very important to the Native people of America. The Iroquois people of the Northeast referred to these vegetables as the "Three Sisters." They believed that the physical and spiritual well-being of their people relied on these sacred sisters, who were the "sustainers of life," gifts from the Creator. Many stories were woven around the sisters who would never be apart from one another. They were planted together, often eaten together, and celebrated together.

Honey–Basted Turkey (Northeast)

Preheat oven to 350 degrees Fahrenheit.

Ingredients:

1 small turkey
2 tablespoons hazelnut or peanut oil
½ teaspoon ground sage
½ teaspoon ground dried allspice
salt and pepper
1 small bunch green onions
3 to 4 tablespoons honey

Cooking utensils you'll need:
measuring spoons
roasting pan
basting brush

Directions:

Remove the *giblets* from the turkey. Rinse the turkey, and dry it, then rub with the oil and season it with salt, pepper, sage, and allspice. Fill the neck and body cavities with onions and *truss* if you want. Place turkey in the roasting pan and allow to cook for at least 18 to 20 minutes per pound. It is done when you prick a thigh with a knife or fork and the resulting juices are clear. During the last hour, baste the turkey with honey. After it is finished, *garnish* with strings of cranberries.

American Indian History and Traditions

When you think of turkey, what's the next thought that comes to mind? If you're like many Americans, it may be "Thanksgiving." In our minds, turkey and Thanksgiving go together the way Christmas and presents do.

But if it weren't for the Native people of Massachusetts, who shared their food lore with the Pilgrim settlers, we might not be celebrating Thanksgiving at all. When the Europeans first arrived on Massachusetts' coast, the new land seemed unfamiliar and unfriendly. Most of them were used to living in the city, and they had no idea how to find food in this cold, rocky land. Helpful Natives—like Squanto and Chief Massasoit—were the ones who showed the settlers that nature could provide them with bountiful feasts: roots, seeds, and berries, as well as turkey and other wildfowl. To celebrate their survival and the blessings they had experienced, the Pilgrims celebrated a harvest festival with their new friends. Turkey was on the menu at that first feast of thanksgiving, just as it still is today.

Indian Pudding (Northeast)

Preheat oven to 300 degrees Fahrenheit.

Ingredients:

4 cups milk
1 cup maple syrup
¼ cup butter
⅔ cup cornmeal
½ teaspoon dried ginger
¼ teaspoon ground nutmeg
1½ cups dried currants or raisins
ice cream (optional)

Cooking utensils you'll need:
measuring cups
measuring spoons
saucepan
casserole
small mixing bowl

Directions:

Grease the casserole. Over medium heat, combine 3 cups of milk and the maple syrup in the saucepan. When it boils, add the butter. Combine the nutmeg, ginger, and cornmeal in a separate bowl. Gradually stir this into the milk mixture and lower the heat. Cool until it is thickened, which should be about 10 minutes. Add the raisins and stir. Place the whole mixture in the casserole and pour the remaining milk over it, but do not stir it in. Bake the pudding for 2½ hours, or until the milk has been absorbed and the top is golden. Serve warm with ice cream.

American Indian Food History and Tradition

Indian pudding was one of the earliest dishes passed along from Native people to the European settlers. Indians ate the dish with meat and vegetables, as part of the main meal of the day, but the settlers enjoyed it as a dessert they could make from ingredients that were readily available.

American Indian History and Traditions

The Algonquian were the ones who created this earliest version of "Cracker Jacks." Children and adults both enjoyed the sweet, sticky treat. When the white settlers arrived on the scene, they were delighted by the exploding grain—and popcorn took its place in American households as a favorite snack.

Maple Popcorn Balls (Northeast)

Ingredients:

¼ cup popping corn
½ tablespoon salt (optional)
1 cup maple syrup
1½ teaspoons butter

Directions:

Pop the corn and season with salt. Heat the syrup and butter over medium heat in a saucepan, stirring constantly until the temperature reaches 250 degrees Fahrenheit or drops form balls when dropped into cold water. Take the pan off the stove and pour the mixture over the popcorn. When it is cool enough to touch, toss the popcorn with syrup and form into balls. Cool on a greased baking sheet.

Cooking utensils you'll need:
measuring spoons
measuring cups
popcorn popper
cooking thermometer (optional)
large mixing bowl
saucepan
baking sheet

Batter Bread (Great Plains)

Preheat oven to 375 degrees Fahrenheit.

Ingredients:

1 quart milk or water
2 cups cornmeal
3 eggs, separated
4 tablespoons melted butter
1½ teaspoons salt
½ teaspoon pepper

Cooking utensils you'll need:
measuring cups
measuring spoons
saucepan
baking dish
mixing bowl
electric mixer

Directions:

Bring milk or water to a boil in a large saucepan over medium heat. Gradually, stir in cornmeal, and cook until thickened, stirring occasionally. Beat in egg yolks, butter, and seasonings. Beat egg whites in a separate bowl until stiff peaks are formed. *Fold* whites into corn mixture and pour into a greased 2-quart baking dish. Bake for 20-30 minutes, until puffy and golden brown. Makes 6 servings.

American Indian Food History

Corn was once as important to the Plains Indians as it was to the other tribes across North America. But when the Cheyenne became buffalo hunters, they left behind their farming. Many of their stories refer to the time when they "lost their corn." Not until the American government sent them to live on reservations did the Cheyenne go back to growing corn, creating dishes like this one.

One old Cheyenne story goes like this:
Long ago, when the Cheyenne still lived in the north, the people were hungry. They searched for buffalo, but there were none to be found. Two of the hunters stumbled into a mysterious spring, where they found themselves in a large cave. There, an old woman was cooking buffalo meat and corn in two pots.

She looked up and smiled at them. "Grandchildren, come here and sit beside me." They sat down, one on each side of her, and told her the people were hungry and that they had come to her for food. She gave them corn from one pot and meat from the other. They ate until they had had enough, and when they were through, the pots were still full. Then she told them to look toward the south, and they saw that the land in that direction was covered with buffalo. She told them to look to the west, and they saw all kinds of animals, large and small, including ponies, though they knew nothing of ponies in those days. She told them to look toward the north, and they saw corn growing everywhere. The old woman said to them, "All this that you have seen shall be yours in the future. Tonight I cause the buffalo to be restored to you. Take this uncooked corn, and plant it every spring in low, moist ground. After it matures, you can feed upon it."

The two men obeyed the old woman, and the people planted corn every year after this. One spring, however, the Cheyenne went on a buffalo hunt. When they returned, they found that some neighboring tribe had stolen their corn. Nothing but stalks remained—not even a kernel for seed. The Cheyenne never succeeded in tracing the robbers or recovering the stolen crop. And it was a long time before they planted any more corn.

American Indian History and Traditions

Native people across North America eat both squash and pumpkin blossoms—but in the Southwest, this flower is important both as a food and as a religious symbol. The squash kachina—a holy spirit—brings rain and health to the Zuni and Hopi. The Pueblo people create squash blossom designs for their sacred ceremonies by winding yarn around a blossom-shaped frame. The design also appears in their jewelry and other artwork.

Fried Squash Blossoms (Southwest)

Ingredients:

2 dozen squash blossoms
4 eggs
½ cup milk
1 teaspoon chili powder
1 teaspoon salt
¼ teaspoon ground cumin
2 to 3 cups finely ground corn meal
oil for deep frying

Cooking utensils you'll need:
measuring cups
measuring spoons
bowl
saucepan
cooking thermometer (optional)

Directions:

Rinse the blossoms very gently and pat them dry. Beat the eggs with the milk, along with the chili powder, salt, and cumin, in a large bowl. Dip the blossoms in this mixture, then coat in cornmeal. Put the blossoms in the refrigerator for about 10 minutes to set the coating. Then, in a saucepan, heat 2 inches of oil until hot (about 350 degrees, if you want to use a cooking thermometer). Fry the blossoms until golden, putting one or two at a time into the pan. Drain on paper towels and keep them warm by putting them in the oven until the rest are finished. Serve right away.

Tip:

When working with hot oil, always be very careful not to burn yourself. Hot oil spits, so protect your clothing and skin from stains and burns. Keep cooking handles turned away from the outside of the stove, so that younger children do not pull the hot oil onto themselves.

Fry Bread (Southwest)

Ingredients:

3 cups flour
2 teaspoons baking powder
1 teaspoon salt
1½ cups warm water or milk
1 tablespoon liquid shortening
oil or shortening for deep frying

Cooking utensils you'll need:
measuring cups
measuring spoons
mixing bowl
pot

Directions:

Combine all ingredients in a mixing bowl except shortening. *Knead* until smooth. Rub shortening over dough and cover with a dishcloth. Let sit for about 30 minutes. Heat several inches of oil in large pot. Then pat out enough dough to fit in your hand in a circle about ⅛ inch thick. Place dough in hot oil and fry until golden brown. Makes 10–12 fry breads.

Tip:

Fry bread can be served with ground beef, salsa, lettuce, and cheese—like a taco. It can also be served with honey or powdered sugar as a dessert.

American Indian Food History

Fry bread is a modern Indian food that is served across America at powwows and other gatherings. Powwows are opportunities for Native people from all tribes to gather together to dance, celebrate, and affirm their cultural identity. A powwow is also a good chance for non-Indians to learn about and enjoy Native culture and heritage.

American Indian History and Traditions

Pumpkins and piñon nuts are both native to the American Southwest; they were already growing here when the Spaniards arrived in the late fifteenth century. The pumpkin provided the Navajo and Pueblo people with a rich source of vitamin A—as well as a handy edible cooking pot for soups. Piñon nuts come from a dwarf pine tree that today still grows on the rocky hills of New Mexico and Arizona.

Pumpkin Piñon Bread (Southwest)

Preheat oven to 350 degrees Fahrenheit.

Ingredients:

1½ cups flour
1 cup pureed cooked pumpkin
¼ cup sugar
½ cup melted butter
2 eggs, beaten
1 teaspoon baking powder
1 teaspoon cinnamon
1 teaspoon nutmeg
½ teaspoon salt
¼ cup piñon nuts

Cooking utensils you'll need:
measuring cups
measuring spoons
mixing bowl
bread pan

Directions:

Combine ingredients in a mixing bowl. Pour batter into a greased 6x9-inch bread pan and bake for 1 hour.

Tips:

If you can't find piñon nuts in your grocery store, try asking for pine nuts or pignoli, the Italian word for the same seed.

You can be sure bread is done if when you insert a knife or a toothpick, it comes out clean.

Feast Day Cookies

Preheat oven to 350 degrees Fahrenheit.

Ingredients:

⅔ cup vegetable shortening
⅔ cup plus ¼ cup sugar
1 egg
2 cups flour
4½ teaspoons baking powder
½ teaspoon vanilla
½ teaspoon anise seed
⅓ cup milk
½ cup piñon nuts, chopped
1 teaspoon cinnamon

Cooking utensils you'll need:
measuring cups
measuring spoons
bowl
cookie sheets
rolling pin
cookie cutters

Directions:

Cream ⅔ cup sugar and shortening in a bowl. Add egg and stir; then mix in flour, baking powder, vanilla, and anise seed. Gradually add milk until the dough is stiff. Mix in the nuts. Roll dough on a lightly floured surface to a half-inch thickness. Cut into shapes with cookie cutters, and sprinkle tops with remaining sugar and cinnamon. Bake on well-greased cookie sheets for 15 minutes. Makes 2 dozen 2-inch cookies.

American Indian Food History

Nineteen separate Pueblo communities are located in New Mexico. These Native peoples speak five unique languages (Tewa, Tiwa, Towa, Keresan, and Zunian), and each celebrates its own "feast day." In many cases, this sacred and joyful celebration is held on the day dedicated to the pueblo's patron saint. (Often, Spanish missionaries assigned these saints so that each pueblo's feast day would coincide with a traditional ceremony that already existed.) The ceremonies usually include traditional dances outdoors, accompanied by singing and drumming, and plenty of food. Visitors are welcome to this part of the celebration, but the feast day will also include private sacred ceremonies in the pueblo's kiva, a round structure for traditional holy rituals. Catholic church services and processions will be a part of the day as well.

In the old days, all outside visitors to a public dance would be offered a meal in a Pueblo home; today, because so many tourists visit these events, such meals are by personal invitation only. If you're lucky enough to get an invitation someday, you can expect to taste these traditional cookies—but in the meantime, make some for yourself!

Fruit Pies (Southwest)

Preheat oven to 400 degrees Fahrenheit.

Ingredients:

piecrust pastry
fruit pie filling
1 egg
1 tablespoon milk

Cooking utensils you'll need:
measuring spoons
baking sheets
fork
pastry brush

Directions:

Cut pastry into 4-inch circles. Place a tablespoon of pie filling on one half of each circle; fold over the other half of the circle; and press a fork around the edge of the half circle to seal. Prick the tops with a fork. Mix egg with milk and brush on tops of the pies. Bake for 15 minutes, until lightly brown. Makes 10 little pies.

Tip:

You can buy ready-made piecrusts at the grocery store.

American Indian History and Traditions

The Pueblo people are famous for their hospitality. Small fruit pies like these are often offered to visitors to their communities, especially on feast days.

Peach Crisp (Southwest)

Preheat oven to 375 degrees Fahrenheit.

Ingredients:

6 large peaches, peeled, pitted, and sliced (5 to 6 cups)
¼ cup granulated sugar
½ teaspoon cinnamon (optional)
¾ cup unbleached flour
¾ cup light brown sugar
¼ teaspoon salt
½ cup butter
2 tablespoons piñon nuts (See tip on page 49.) (optional)

Cooking utensils you'll need:
measuring cups
measuring spoons
baking dish
mixing bowl

Directions:

Toss the peaches with the sugar and cinnamon in the baking dish. In the bowl, combine the salt, brown sugar, and flour. **Cut** in the butter until the mixture in the bowl looks like coarse meal. Sprinkle this over the peaches, and sprinkle nuts over that. Bake for 30 to 40 minutes, or until golden brown.

American Indian Food History

This recipe comes from the Navajo people. Before the coming of the Spanish, the Navajo ate mostly corn, beans, squash, yucca, and melons, but after the Spaniards' arrival, the Navajo learned new ways to grow food. Metal tools made farming easier, and they learned to plant wheat and potatoes—and peaches. They dried the fruit in the sun, preserving it for the winter months.

The sun was very important to the Navajo, who lived in hogans with doors that faced east, so people could welcome the sun every morning.

American Indian History and Traditions

The forests of southeastern North America were home to the
Choctaw, the Chickasaw, the Creek, the Seminole, and the
Cherokee (often referred to by Europeans as the "Five Civilized
Tribes"). The women of these tribes were creative gardeners
and gatherers, and their meals were based around corn, nuts,
and berries. When white Americans forced these tribes to leave
their homes and relocate in Oklahoma, they brought with them
their food traditions and adapted them to their new surround-
ings.

 Combining carrots with traditional cornbread makes a moist
bread that's rich in vitamin A.

Carrot Bread (Southeast)

Preheat oven to 375 degrees Fahrenheit.

Ingredients:

1 pound carrots, peeled and grated
1¼ cups milk
1¼ cups flour
1¼ cups cornmeal
1½ teaspoons baking powder
2 eggs, beaten
2 tablespoons melted butter
½ cup honey
½ cup dried blueberries or raisins

Cooking utensils you'll need:
measuring cups
measuring spoons
saucepan
mixing bowl
loaf pan

Directions:

Place carrots in a saucepan with milk and bring to a boil. Reduce heat and *simmer* for 5 minutes, stirring. Remove from heat, cool, and pour into a mixing bowl. Add other ingredients. Pour batter into a 5x9-inch greased loaf pan. Bake for 60–70 minutes, until a toothpick inserted into the center of the bread comes out clean.

Steamed Fiddleheads (Northwest)

These curled fronds taste a little like a cross between asparagus and broccoli.

Ingredients:

6 cups fiddlehead ferns
2 to 3 tablespoons melted butter or olive oil
salt and pepper to taste

Cooking utensils you'll need:
measuring cups
measuring spoons
sauce pan

Directions:

Rinse fiddleheads and **blanch** or steam for 3 to 4 minutes. Toss with the oil and season with salt and pepper.

Tip:

Fiddleheads are in season in early spring. You can often find them in your grocery store. Look for tightly curled fern fronds that will be tender to eat.

American Indian Food History

Native Americans on both the east and west coasts enjoy fiddleheads as a spring treat—but ferns were particularly important to the people who lived in the moist Northwest. Not only
did they eat the fiddleheads in the spring, but fern roots served
as a starchy vegetable (a little like potatoes) all year round, a
rare treat for these people in the days before the coming of the
Europeans. The raw roots were also chewed as cough medicine,
and fern fronds were used as mats and bedding. When the
salmon began to run in the spring, ferns also played a part in
the welcoming ceremony.

American Indian History and Traditions

Native Americans feasted from nature's table. Many varieties of tender young plants and flowers added fiber and vitamins to their menus in the spring and summer. Today, many of our garden plants—like watercress and nasturtiums—are cultivated descendents of plants with which Indians have been familiar for centuries.

Wild Greens and Flowers Salad (Northwest)

Ingredients:

1 cup watercress leaves and tender stems
1 cup lamb's-quarter (also called pitseed, goosefoot, or pigweed) or small spinach leaves and tender stems
1 cup arugula or tender dandelion leaves
½ cup tender nasturtium and violet leaves and flowers
1 tablespoon honey
¼ cup cider vinegar
⅓ cup sunflower or corn oil
2 teaspoons chopped fresh mint or dill weed
salt and pepper (optional)

Cooking utensils you'll need:
measuring cups
measuring spoons
salad bowl

Directions:

Rinse the greens and flowers. Combine the honey, oil, and vinegar in a bowl and add mint, salt, and pepper to season. Add the greens and toss.

Tip:

If you can't find these greens growing wild, you can make this salad with "field greens" available from your grocery store—and if you can get permission to pick the flowers from a garden or lawn, they will add color and beauty to the salad (as well as flavor).

Blackberry Cobbler (Southeast)

Preheat oven to 375 degrees Fahrenheit.

Ingredients:

⅓ cup milk
1 egg, beaten
2 tablespoons melted butter
1 teaspoon baking powder
¾ teaspoon salt
1¼ cups cornmeal
¾ cup honey
1 quart fresh or frozen blackberries

Cooking utensils you'll need:
measuring cups
measuring spoons
mixing bowl
baking dish

Directions:

Combine milk, egg, butter, baking powder, and salt in a mixing bowl. Stir in cornmeal and ½ cup honey. Place berries in the bottom of a buttered baking dish and spoon remaining honey over them. Drop batter by tablespoons over berries and bake for 30–35 minutes, until berries are bubbling and crust is golden. Makes 6 servings.

American Indian Food History

Native people across North America enjoyed the sweetness berries brought to their foods. This recipe comes from the Creek people, descendents of the great Muscogee Confederacy that once spread across southeastern North America. Eventually, the U.S. government pushed these people onto a small reservation in Oklahoma, while others settled in Alabama. Like other Native American groups, the Creek have faced great hardship—but traditional foods are just one thing that helps them keep alive a dynamic spirituality and worldview that gives them courage and hope.

Further Reading

Buchanan, Carol. *Brother Crow, Sister Corn: Traditional American Indian Gardening*. New York: Ten Speed Press, 1997.

Caduto, Michael J. and Joseph Bruchac. *Native American Gardening: Stories, Projects, and Recipes for Families*. New York: Fulcrum, 1996.

Carew-Miller, Anna. *Native American Cooking*. Philadelphia, Penn.: Mason Crest, 2002.

Gunderson, Mary and E. Barrie Kavasch. *American Indian Cooking Before 1500 (Exploring History Through Simple Recipes)*. New York: Capstone, 2000.

Hughes, Phyllis. *Pueblo Indian Cookbook: Recipes from the Pueblos of the American Southwest*. Santa Fe: Museum of New Mexico Press, 1997.

Keoke, Emory Dean and Kay Marie Porterfield. *Encyclopedia of American Indian Contributions to the World*. New York: Facts on File, 2002.

Sanna, Ellyn. *Food Folklore*. Philadelphia, Penn.: Mason Crest Publishers, 2003.

For More Information

Encyclopedia of North American Indians—Food and Cuisine
College.hmco.com/history/readerscomp/naind/html/na_012400_foodand-
cuisi.htm

How American Indians used their environment to find food
www.fcps.k12.va.us/DeerParkES/kids/whiting/American%20Indian%20tem-
plate.htm

Native American foods
www.nativetech.org/food/

Native American recipes
www.kstrom.net/isk/food/recipes.html
mypeoplepc.com/members/cherlyn/onefeather/id5.html

Traditional American Indian recipes
www.folkart.com/newsletter/0100/page3.htm

Publisher's note:
The Web sites listed on this page were active at the time of publication. The publisher is not responsible for Web sites that have changed their addresses or discon-
tinued operation since the date of publication. The publisher will review and update
the Web sites upon each reprint.

Index

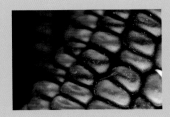

Author:

Ellyn Sanna is the author of *101 Easy Supper Recipes for Busy Moms* from Promise Press, and several recipe gift books from Barbour Publishing, including *Feast, An Invitation to Tea,* and the books in the "Christmas at Home" series. A former middle school teacher and the mother of three children ages eleven through sixteen, she has experience addressing both the learning needs and the food tastes of young cooks. Ellyn Sanna has also authored and edited numerous educational titles.

Recipe Tester / Food Preparer:

Marsha McIntosh is a gifted cook who has studied and worked with American Indians across the United States. She and her husband worked together on eight books for the Mason Crest series, North American Indians Today, traveling across the country to interview Native groups. They live in Flagstaff, Arizona, near the Navajo and Hopi reservations.

Consultant:

The Culinary Institute of America is considered the world's premier culinary college. It is a private, not-for-profit learning institution, dedicated to providing the world's best culinary education. Its campuses in New York and California provide learning environments that focus on excellence, leadership, professionalism, ethics, and respect for diversity. The institute embodies a passion for food with first-class cooking expertise.

Recipe Contributor:

Alfred Herron is both a cook and a teacher. He is a Seneca Indian with an interest in Native recipes.

Picture Credits

Corel: p. 22
Dover: cover
PhotoDisc: cover, pp. 13, 32
Photos.Com: pp. 10, 13, 16, 20, 26, 27, 38, 43, 44, 57, 61, 68, 72
Benjamin Stewart: cover, pp. 9, 13, 16, 17, 19, 25, 29, 31, 35, 37, 41, 47, 48, 51, 52, 54, 58, 62, 65, 68, 69